Spotlight on Songwriters

PHOEBE BRIDGERS

Ursula Pang

CREATED BY Humans

Published in 2027 by The Rosen Publishing Group, Inc.
2544 Clinton Street, Buffalo, NY 14224

First Edition

Editor: Greg Roza
Designer: Michael Flynn

Photo Credits: Cover SOPA Images Limited/Alamy Live News; (series background) Yuliya Chsherbakova/Shutterstock.com; p. 5 Tinseltown/Shutterstock.com; p. 7 https://commons.wikimedia.org/wiki/File:Sloppy_Jane_(8630792762).jpg; pp. 9, 17 Daniel DeSlover/ZUMA Wire/Alamy; p. 11 Greg Chow/ZUMA Wire/Alamy Live News; p. 13 https://commons.wikimedia.org/wiki/File:Phoebe_Bridgers_-_Theater_Roode_Bioscope,_Amsterdam_-_2017.jpg; pp. 15, 19, 21 Ben Houdijk/Shutterstock.com.

Cataloging-in-Publication Data

Names: Pang, Ursula.
Title: Phoebe Bridgers / Ursula Pang.
Description: Buffalo, New York : Created by Humans, an imprint of Rosen Publishing, 2027. | Series: Spotlight on songwriters| Includes glossary and index.
Identifiers: ISBN 9781534553491 (pbk.) | ISBN 9781534553507 (library bound) | ISBN 9781534553514 (ebook)
Subjects: LCSH: Bridgers, Phoebe, 1994---Juvenile literature. | Singer-songwriters--United States--Biography--Juvenile literature. | Rock musicians--United States--Biography--Juvenile literature.
Classification: LCC ML3930.B75 P36 2027 | DDC 782.42166092--dc23

Manufactured in the United States of America

CPSIA Compliance Information: Batch #CSCBH27. For Further Information contact Rosen Publishing at 1-800-237-9932.

CONTENTS

Young Musician

Phoebe Bridgers was born on August 17, 1994. She grew up in Pasadena, California. Her mom was a **comedian**. Her dad built sets for TV shows and movies. Phoebe started learning music at an early age. She began playing guitar when she was just 13.

Phoebe Bridgers
Jamie Bridgers

Getting Started

Phoebe went to the Los Angeles County High School for the Arts. She practiced jazz singing. She started performing for crowds when she was just a teenager. Her first shows were at a local farmers market! She also performed in coffee shops around Los Angeles, California.

Breaking Out

In 2014, Phoebe made a short album titled "Killer." Singer and songwriter Ryan Adams met Phoebe and was impressed with her talent. He released "Killer" through his own record company, PAX AM. This helped Phoebe to reach more people with her music.

Works Well with Others

Phoebe released the song "Smoke Signals" in 2017. This led to larger shows for her. She sang in concerts with Ryan Adams and singer-songwriter Conor Oberst. This was a great honor for Phoebe. She had been a fan of Oberst for years.

Conor Oberst

Stranger in the Alps

Phoebe released her first full-length album in 2017. *Stranger in the Alps* proved that Phoebe was a talented musician and songwriter. The songs on this album are deeply personal. Some music **critics** called the album "sad **folk music**" although most people call it "**indie rock**."

Supergroups

Phoebe has worked with many other talented singer-songwriters. She is a member of the band boygenius with Lucy Dacus and Julien Baker. They have two popular albums: *Boygenius* and *The Record*. Phoebe and Conor Oberst also formed a band called Better Oblivion Community Center.

BOYGENIUS

Punisher

In 2020, Phoebe released her second album titled *Punisher*. It was a huge hit with fans and critics! It was **nominated** for four **Grammy Awards**, but did not win. Still, the album was considered one of the best to be released in 2020. Phoebe's fame was growing.

Award Winner!

In 2024, Phoebe and her group boygenius won three Grammy Awards for the album *The Record*. The song "Not Strong Enough" won for Best Rock Song and Best Rock Performance. Phoebe and the rap star SZA also won Best Pop/Duo Group Performance for the song "Ghost in the Machine."

Super Songwriter!

Phoebe continues to work with other singer-songwriters including Taylor Swift and Lorde. Her music has been featured in TV shows and movies. She likes to put on surprise concerts for her fans. Phoebe has been called one of the greatest songwriters in the world today!

GLOSSARY

comedian: Someone paid to tell jokes to crowds.

critic: Someone who judges the value or worth of something, such as music, movies, food, etc.

folk music: A type of music based on traditional musical styles that does not use electric instruments.

Grammy Awards: Prizes given every year in the United States for the people who create music.

indie rock: A term for bands that make rock music without the help of large record companies. Short for "independent rock."

nominate: To choose someone who you think deserves an award.

FOR MORE INFORMATION

BOOKS

Edwards, Sue Bradford. *Making Music*. North Mankato, MN: Essential Library, 2024.

Kington, Emily. *Be the Best at Guitar.* Cornwall, UK: Hungry Tomato, 2024.

WEBSITES

Phoebe Bridgers
www.grammy.com/artists/phoebe-bridgers/287153/
Visit this webpage to learn more about Phoebe's Grammy Award wins and nominations.

Songwriters Hall of Fame
www.songhall.org
Read about the greatest songwriters of all time.

INDEX